STEPS TO GROWING YOUR SMALL BUSINESS

STEPS TO SCALING YOUR SMALL BUSINESS TO SUCCESS

By Linda N Newell

TABLE OF CONTENT

CHAPTER ONE

Introduction

Small businesses are the backbone of the economy. According to the Small Business Administration (SBA), small businesses make up 99.9% of all U.S. businesses and employ nearly half of the private sector workforce. Small businesses are crucial drivers of innovation, job creation, and economic growth.

Starting a small business can be challenging, but it can also be very rewarding. Some common challenges include securing funding, navigating regulatory requirements, and developing a competitive advantage in a crowded marketplace. However, small business owners also enjoy a great deal of flexibility, autonomy, and control over their work.

Small businesses come in many different forms. Some are sole proprietorships, where the owner is the sole operator of the business. Others are partnerships, where two or more people share ownership and responsibility. Still others are corporations or LLCs, which offer various legal and tax benefits.

Marketing is a critical component of small business success. Effective marketing can help you reach your target audience, build brand awareness, and differentiate yourself from competitors. Some effective marketing strategies for small businesses include social media marketing, email marketing, content marketing, and networking.

Small businesses need to be agile and adaptable in order to survive and thrive. The business landscape is constantly evolving, and small businesses must be able to pivot quickly in response to changing market conditions or customer needs. This requires a willingness to take risks, experiment with new ideas, and learn from both successes and failures.

Small businesses can benefit from a variety of resources and support services. The SBA offers a range of programs and resources for small business owners, including business counseling, training and education, and access to capital. Local economic development organizations, chambers of commerce, and industry associations can also provide valuable support and networking opportunities.

Small business owners should prioritize their own personal and professional development. Running a small business can be stressful and demanding, and it is important to take care of yourself both physically and mentally. This may include setting aside time for exercise, hobbies, or other activities that bring you joy, as well as seeking out opportunities for personal or professional growth.

Small businesses should prioritize customer satisfaction. Providing excellent customer service and building strong relationships with customers is essential for building loyalty and generating repeat business. This may involve responding promptly to customer inquiries and concerns, offering personalized recommendations and solutions, and regularly soliciting feedback and input from customers.

Small businesses should also prioritize employee satisfaction. Happy and engaged employees are more productive, committed, and likely to provide excellent customer service. This may involve offering competitive salaries and benefits, providing opportunities for professional development and growth, and fostering a positive and supportive work environment.

Small businesses should stay informed about industry trends and best practices. Keeping up-to-date on the latest developments in your industry can help you stay competitive and identify new opportunities for growth. This may involve attending industry conferences, subscribing to relevant publications or newsletters, or participating in online forums or discussion groups.

Small businesses should also prioritize sustainability and social responsibility. Consumers are increasingly concerned about issues like climate change, ethical sourcing, and social justice, and small businesses can differentiate themselves by demonstrating a commitment to these values. This may involve adopting environmentally friendly practices, supporting local charities or community organizations, or prioritizing fair labor practices and ethical sourcing.

Small businesses are essential drivers of economic growth and innovation, but they also face a number of challenges in a crowded and constantly evolving marketplace. By prioritizing customer and employee satisfaction, staying informed about industry trends, and demonstrating a commitment to sustainability and social responsibility, small businesses can build a strong foundation for long-term success.

CHAPTER TWO

Some Risks associated with starting up a business

Starting a business is a challenging and rewarding endeavor, but it also comes with a number of risks. Here are some common risks associated with starting up a business:

Financial risk: Starting a business requires significant financial investment, and there is always the risk that you will not be able to generate enough revenue to cover your expenses. This can lead to debt, bankruptcy, or even personal financial ruin.

Market risk: Even if you have a great idea for a product or service, there is always the risk that the market will not be receptive to it. This can be due to factors like changing consumer preferences, economic downturns, or increased competition.

Operational risk: Running a business involves a wide range of operational tasks, from managing employees to handling logistics and supply chain issues. There is always the risk that something will go wrong, whether it's a supply chain disruption, a product defect, or a data breach.

Legal and regulatory risk: Businesses must comply with a wide range of laws and regulations, from employment laws to tax codes to environmental regulations. Failure to comply with these regulations can result in fines, lawsuits, and other legal and financial consequences.

Reputation risk: In today's interconnected world, a business's reputation is more important than ever. Negative reviews or publicity can quickly spread on social media, leading to damage to the brand and loss of customers.

Personal risk: Starting a business can be incredibly stressful and time-consuming, and can take a toll on your personal life and relationships. There is also the risk that you will have to sacrifice your personal financial stability and security in order to invest in the business.

While these risks may seem daunting, it's important to remember that many successful businesses have started out with similar risks and challenges. By doing thorough research, developing a solid business plan, and seeking out support from mentors and advisors, you can mitigate these risks and increase your chances of success.

CHAPTER THREE

Practical plan that will help my small business yield within six months

As a small business owner, you are likely always looking for ways to increase revenue and improve profitability. One way to achieve this is to implement a practical plan that focuses on a combination of marketing, customer service, and operations. Here is a six-month practical plan that can help your small business yield:

Month 1: Define Your Target Audience

The first step in any marketing plan is to define your target audience. This involves identifying the demographic characteristics of your ideal customer, including age, gender, income, and interests. Once you have a clear picture of your target audience, you can tailor your marketing efforts to appeal to them specifically.

Month 2: Build Your Online Presence

In today's digital age, having a strong online presence is crucial for any small business. This involves creating a professional website, setting up social media accounts, and ensuring that your business is listed on relevant directories such as Google My Business. A strong online presence can help attract new customers and build brand awareness.

Month 3: Improve Your Customer Service

Customer service is a key factor in customer retention and satisfaction. Take this month to focus on improving your customer service by training your employees to provide exceptional service, responding promptly to customer inquiries, and implementing a feedback system to gather insights on areas for improvement.

Month 4: Launch a Promotional Campaign

To attract new customers and drive sales, consider launching a promotional campaign. This could include offering discounts, hosting a special event, or launching a referral program. Be sure to promote your campaign through your website and social media accounts to reach your target audience.

Month 5: Streamline Your Operations

To increase efficiency and reduce costs, take this month to review your operations and identify areas for improvement. This could include automating certain processes, implementing inventory management systems, or optimizing your supply chain. Streamlining your operations can help free up time and resources to focus on growing your business.

Month 6: Measure Your Results

The final month of the plan is dedicated to measuring your results. Review your revenue and profit margins to determine whether your plan has been successful. If you have achieved your goals, consider continuing with the plan or adjusting it to focus on new areas for growth. If you have not achieved your goals, identify areas for improvement and adjust your plan accordingly.

In implementing a practical plan that focuses on marketing, customer service, and operations can help your small business yield within six months. By defining your target audience, building your online presence, improving your customer service, launching a promotional campaign, streamlining your operations, and measuring your results, you can set your business on a path to success. Remember that success doesn't happen overnight, but by consistently executing your plan, you can achieve your goals and grow your business.

CHAPTER FOUR

How to professionalize your small business so it succeeds

Running a small business can be a challenging endeavor, but with the right approach and strategies, it can be a successful venture. One of the critical steps to achieving success in a small business is professionalizing it. Professionalizing a small business means taking steps to make it more efficient, organized, and effective in delivering its products or services to customers. Here are some tips on how to professionalize your small business so that it succeeds:

Establish a clear vision and mission

One of the first steps to professionalizing your small business is to establish a clear vision and mission. This will help you define your business goals and align them with your values, making it easier for you to make decisions and communicate effectively with your team and customers.

Invest in technology

Investing in technology is a crucial step in professionalizing your small business. It will help you automate tasks, increase efficiency, and streamline your operations. This could include software for accounting, project management, customer relationship management (CRM), and other areas where automation can make a significant difference.

Develop a strong brand identity

Developing a strong brand identity is essential for any business looking to succeed. This involves creating a consistent look and feel for your business across all marketing materials, including your logo, website, social media profiles, and other communication channels. A strong brand identity helps to build trust with customers and makes it easier for them to recognize and remember your business.

Hire the right people

Hiring the right people is essential for professionalizing your small business. Look for candidates with the right skills and experience, as well as a passion for your industry and a commitment to your business goals. Hiring the right people will help you build a strong team and create a positive work culture, which is critical for attracting and retaining customers.

Develop effective processes

Developing effective processes is key to professionalizing your small business. This means identifying the steps involved in delivering your products or services and streamlining them to increase efficiency and reduce costs. This could include implementing quality control measures, creating standard operating procedures, and developing a customer service plan.

Monitor and measure performance

Monitoring and measuring performance is critical to professionalizing your small business. This involves setting clear performance metrics and regularly tracking and analyzing your progress towards your goals. This will help you identify areas for improvement and make data-driven decisions that can help you grow your business.

Focus on customer service

Finally, focusing on customer service is essential for professionalizing your small business. This means putting your customers first and ensuring that they have an excellent experience every time they interact with your business. This could involve implementing a customer feedback system, training your staff to be attentive to customer needs, and resolving customer complaints quickly and effectively.

Professionalizing your small business is crucial for success. By following the tips outlined above, you can develop a strong vision and mission, invest in technology, build a strong brand identity, hire the right people, develop effective processes, monitor and measure performance, and focus on customer service. With these strategies in place, you can set your small business up for success and achieve your goals.

Growing small business requires a lot of hard work, dedication, and careful planning. There are several steps that small business owners can take to increase their chances of success. Firstly, identifying a clear target market and establishing a strong brand identity can help attract and retain customers. Secondly, investing in technology and developing effective processes can improve efficiency and reduce costs. Thirdly, hiring the right people and providing them with the necessary training and support can create a positive work culture and boost productivity. Finally, monitoring performance and making data-driven decisions can help identify areas for improvement and drive growth. By following these steps and remaining adaptable to changing market conditions, small business owners can build a successful and sustainable enterprise.

Ultimately, growing a small business is a journey that requires patience and resilience. It is important to remain focused on the long-term goals and to be prepared to adapt to new challenges along the way. As the business grows, it may become necessary to seek outside funding, expand into new markets, and form partnerships with other businesses. However, it is important not to lose sight of the core values and mission that drove the business in the first place. By staying true to these principles and continually striving to improve, small business owners can build a thriving enterprise that provides value to its customers and contributes to the wider community.

CHAPTER FIVE

"Do's and Don'ts for Small Business Owners."

As an entrepreneur starting a small business, it can be challenging to navigate the ins and outs of running a successful company. There are many factors to consider, from finances to marketing to employee management. In this essay, we'll cover some of the most important "Do's and Don'ts" that small business owners should keep in mind.

DO: Research your market

Before starting any business, it's essential to research your market thoroughly. You need to understand your target audience, their needs, and the competition in your industry. This research will help you identify your unique selling proposition (USP), which is what sets your business apart from others.

When researching your market, you should also consider factors like pricing, customer service, and marketing strategies. This information will help you develop a comprehensive business plan that outlines how you will compete in your industry.

DON'T: Neglect your finances

One of the most common reasons small businesses fail is because they neglect their finances. As a business owner, you need to understand your cash flow, budget, and financial projections. You should also set aside money for unexpected expenses and emergencies.

To stay on top of your finances, it's a good idea to hire an accountant or bookkeeper. They can help you keep track of your expenses, pay your taxes on time, and manage your cash flow.

DO: Build a strong brand

Building a strong brand is essential for any small business. Your brand represents who you are and what you stand for, and it's what customers will remember about your business. Your brand should be consistent across all marketing channels, including your website, social media, and advertising.

To build a strong brand, you should consider factors like your company's values, mission, and personality. You should also invest in quality branding materials, such as a logo and website design. A strong brand will help you stand out in a crowded market and attract loyal customers.

DON'T: Ignore customer feedback

Customers are the lifeblood of any small business, and it's essential to listen to their feedback. Your customers can provide valuable insights into what's working and what's not, and they can help you identify areas for improvement.

To collect customer feedback, you can use surveys, online reviews, and social media. It's also a good idea to respond to customer feedback promptly and professionally. This shows your customers that you value their opinions and are committed to providing the best possible service.

DO: Hire the right employees

Hiring the right employees is essential for any small business. Your employees are the face of your company, and they can make or break your customer experience. When hiring employees, you should look for candidates who share your company's values and are committed to providing excellent customer service.

To attract the best candidates, you should offer competitive wages, benefits, and opportunities for growth. You should also invest in employee training and development to help your team reach their full potential.

DON'T: Overextend yourself

One of the biggest mistakes small business owners make is overextending themselves. This can happen when you take on too much work, hire too many employees, or invest too much money into your business. Overextending yourself can lead to burnout, financial stress, and poor business decisions.

To avoid overextending yourself, it's important to set realistic goals and manage your workload. You should also prioritize self-care and take time off when needed. Remember that running a successful business is a marathon, not a sprint.

DO: Embrace technology

In today's digital age, technology is essential for any small business. From social media marketing to online sales, technology can help you reach new customers and grow your business. You should embrace technology and stay up to date with the latest tools and trends in your industry.

Some examples of technology that small businesses can use include:

Social media: Social media platforms like Facebook, Instagram, and Twitter can help you reach new customers and build brand awareness. You can use social media to share updates about your business, promote special offers, and engage with your audience.

E-commerce platforms: E-commerce platforms like Shopify and WooCommerce can help you set up an online store and sell products online. This can be a great way to reach customers who prefer to shop online.

Project management tools: Project management tools like Asana and Trello can help you stay organized and manage your workload. These tools can be especially helpful if you have a team of employees or contractors.

Cloud storage: Cloud storage services like Google Drive and Dropbox can help you store and access your business files from anywhere. This can be a great way to stay organized and collaborate with others.

DON'T: Skimp on marketing

Marketing is essential for any small business, and it's important to invest in marketing strategies that work. You should consider factors like your target audience, budget, and marketing goals when developing a marketing plan.

Some marketing strategies that small businesses can use include:

Content marketing: Content marketing involves creating valuable content, like blog posts and videos, to attract and engage your audience. This can help you build trust and establish yourself as an authority in your industry.

Email marketing: Email marketing involves sending targeted emails to your subscribers to promote your products or services. This can be a great way to build relationships with your audience and drive sales.

Paid advertising: Paid advertising involves paying to promote your business, like through Google Ads or Facebook Ads. This can be a great way to reach new customers and drive traffic to your website.
DO: Adapt to change

The business world is constantly evolving, and it's important to adapt to change to stay relevant. You should be open to new ideas and willing to try new strategies to grow your business.

Some examples of how small businesses can adapt to change include:

Offering new products or services: You can expand your business by offering new products or services that appeal to your target audience.

Embracing new technology: As mentioned earlier, technology can help you reach new customers and grow your business. You should be open to new tools and trends in your industry.

Changing your marketing strategy: If your current marketing strategy isn't working, you should be willing to try something new. This might involve shifting your focus to a different marketing channel or targeting a different audience.

DON'T: Neglect your work-life balance

As a small business owner, it can be easy to get caught up in work and neglect your personal life. However, it's important to prioritize your work-life balance to avoid burnout and maintain your well-being.

Some tips for maintaining a healthy work-life balance include:

Setting boundaries: You should establish clear boundaries between your work and personal life. This might involve setting specific work hours or avoiding work-related tasks during your personal time.

Prioritizing self-care: You should prioritize activities that help you relax and recharge, like exercise, meditation, or spending time with loved ones.

Delegating tasks: If you have employees or contractors, you should delegate tasks to lighten your workload and avoid overextending yourself.

Starting a small business can be challenging, but by keeping these do's and don'ts in mind, you can increase your chances of success. Remember to research your market, manage your finances, build a strong brand, listen to customer feedback, hire the right employees, embrace technology, invest in marketing, adapt to change, and prioritize your work-life balance. With these tips, you can build a thriving small business and achieve your entrepreneurial dreams.

www.ingramcontent.com/pod-product-compliance
Lightning Source LLC
Chambersburg PA
CBHW071146220526
45467CB00015B/2038